FINEST KNOWN
EXQUISITE HISTORIC RARITIES

Dear Ancient Coin Enthusiast,

Thank you for your recent purchase of Gold Coins of Ancient Rome—First and Second Edition. We're thrilled by the overwhelming response to this offer, a clear indication of the growing interest and passion in the ancient coin market.

Enclosed, you'll find:

- Your First Edition copy of Gold Coins of Ancient Rome.
- A stunning Flavian Dynasty pure silver denarius—a prized addition to any collection.

Exciting News!

The highly anticipated Second Edition of Gold Coins of Ancient Rome is set for release in March. As a valued customer, your name is already on file, and **we'll ship the expanded version to you as soon as it's available.**

A Rare Opportunity Awaits You!

Your name has been entered into our exclusive drawing for the 2024 restrike of the ultra-rare Octavian Divus Julius aureus. This historic coin is a collector's dream! **The winner will be announced on January 31**. Want to learn more? Simply scan the QR code included to explore the remarkable history of this legendary piece.

Special Discount for You!

As a token of our appreciation, we're offering **a $150 discount on any purchase of $500 or more** from our ancient coin collection. Browse our current listings by scanning the QR code—it's the perfect chance to expand your collection with rare and exquisite finds.

Sell or Expand Your Collection with Us!

Finest Known actively seeks ancient coins of exceptional quality and rarity. Whether you're looking to sell or expand your collection, we'd love to assist. Feel free to call or email us at **acrum@finestknown.com**.

Thank you for your trust and enthusiasm. We're honored to be part of your numismatic journey and look forward to serving you again.

Sincerely,

Adam J. Crum
Finest Known

SCAN ME

SESTERTIUS

DENARIUS

AUREUS

Call **888-751-1933**
or view images on
www.FinestKnown.com

Gold Coins of Ancient Rome
Featuring the XII Caesars Legacy Collection

~ CONTENTS ~

~ ACKNOWLEDGEMENTS ~

Karl Newman

Adam Holt

Max Minshull

Ryan Dempsey

Balazs Csaki

~ FOREWORD ~

The pursuit of collecting ancient Roman coins creates a legacy rich in historical intrigue and a lasting store of wealth. Western, Middle Eastern, and North African civilizations are deeply rooted in what we remember as the Roman Empire. Today collectors, numismatic scholars, and history buffs are inspired by these little works of art.

For thousands of collectors and investors, the contributions of Adam Crum to the world of rare and historical gold coins form a foundation that can assist a collector of any level. His countless published articles, many contributions to numismatic books, and his own authored books have entertained, inspired, and stimulated thousands of collectors for decades.

In this book, Adam takes you on a historical journey from the beginnings of Julius Caesar's rule in 44 BC to the end of the Flavian Dynasty in AD 96. I believe any reader interested in historically significant rarities will be inspired to seek out more in-depth tales that these coins rich in history have inspired.

The amazing set highlighted in this little book is a beautiful example of a Twelve Caesars collection that can be assembled with patience and perseverance. Each coin within is a true rarity of museum quality and the entire collection is one in which a legacy can be formed.

The set also represents the first time, to my knowledge, that an LLC partnership was formed to acquire an ancient coin collection, or any rare coin collection. There are eight partners in the LLC that was formed to acquire these amazing works of art struck in gold. Each hoping these amazing artifacts of the ancient world continue their impressive rise in value under their custodianship. Which is in fact all we are as collectors; we are trusted custodians for an asset that will continue to endure the test of time.

I have had the unique opportunity and pleasure of building many sets of these historical coins in gold, silver, and bronze. The superb coins within this set of 12 gold aurei is the second finest I have had the privilege to be involved and one of the Top 5 sets that can be assembled today.

Having this book on your coffee table is a must for every collector looking to take on the extreme challenge of completing a set of Twelve Caesars. I, for one, will enjoy referring to it time and time again.

Lee Minshull
Professional Numismatist
and Collector

IDES OF MARCH

The Death of Julius Caesar (1806) by Vincenzo Camuccini ~ *Public Domain* ~

GOLD AUREUS JULIUS CAESAR ASSASSINATION COIN
SOLD FOR $4.2 MILLION IN OCTOBER 2020

~ INTRODUCTION ~

In all great civilizations, ideas are born from strife and heartache. In ancient Rome, rivaling philosophies led to civil wars, political and military conquests, and assassinations that resulted in one of the greatest empires the world has ever seen. Famed Roman citizen and historian Gaius Suetonius Tranquillus, circa AD 71-135, wrote his famous work, 'De Vita Caesarium,' which translates literally from Latin to "About the Life of the Caesars." He chronicled the biographies of the Roman Empire's twelve Caesars, covering Rome's history from 49 BC to AD 96, capturing forever the lives of the founding men who began an empire that remains the most famous empire of Western Civilization. From narcissistic to sadistic, from humble to kind, their legacies live on forever as works of art sculpted onto tangible gold, silver, copper, and bronze artifacts direct from their golden age. Much of what we know about our world and its origins is because of coinage, and there is truly no better way to begin a coin collection than with the Twelve Caesars.

As a professional numismatist, I have been studying and collecting rare coins of all types for decades, but ancient coins, specifically those from the early Roman Empire, are especially near and dear to my heart. There is a good reason for this: These coins are exceedingly rare, particularly those in investment grade condition and they have had an outstanding track record of not only maintaining value over the years, but steadily increasing in value over time. In fact, selected rare coins from early Roman times have increased in value no less than five-fold, just in the last decade alone!

In addition, coins from the Roman empire have great historical significance. Each is a time capsule exposing the political, social, and financial landscape of the time of the great Caesars of Rome. Holding one of these rare pieces of history in your hands is a delight, every coin is a wonder to behold. So, it should be no surprise that these ancient rarities have exploded in popularity in recent years, and now represent what I believe to be one of the greatest opportunities in all of numismatics today.

This special group of ancient Roman coins, hand-struck during the time of the ''Twelve Caesars,'' from 49 BC through AD 96, takes you through the reign of Julius Caesar all the way to the reign of the last of the Flavian emperors, Domitian.

The amazing set featured on the pages of this book will thrill not only the most astute collectors and investors, but it will bring to life the history and intrigue of the leaders whose images are portrayed on each superb example. The specimens representing each of the Twelve Caesars adorning the pages that follow represent the very best in quality and eye appeal.

For those who strive for a strategic storage of wealth and diversification, I believe the opportunity in these ancient rarities is exceptional. This market segment has mass global appeal due to the influence of the Roman Empire which can be seen across the Eurasian continent and much of the Americas to this day. Add to that, the confidence of third-party grading and certification which has achieved global recognition, this exciting and historical market segment is poised to continue to expand its space in a global marketplace.

Adam J. Crum
Professional Numismatist

ANCIENT ROME TODAY

The Flavian Amphitheater Known as the Roman Colosseum and the Arch of Titus ~ *Credit, Royalty Free ~*

~ THE XII CAESARS ~

Few civilizations throughout history have made such a profound impact on the human story as that of the Twelve Caesars of the Roman empire. The reign of the Twelve Caesars has inspired countless books, movies, and visitors drawn to the historic archaeological sites of the Ancient Greco-Roman world. These emperors engineered Rome's transformation from a Republic to a hereditary monarchy. There is detailed documentation of their lives preserved for history by such biographers as Suetonius and Tacitus at the time. These men of ancient history ruled in a formative and volatile time, from the collapse of the Republic, civil war, and to the rise of an empire that dominated the Mediterranean and most of Europe.

Julius Caesar played a critical role in the demise of the Roman Republic and the rise of the Roman Empire. Augustus was the first Roman emperor and established the empire. Tiberius reigned during the times of Christ and is mentioned in the Bible. Caligula, Claudius, and Nero are all infamous emperors known for their eccentricities and brutality. These six Rulers comprised the first period, known as the Julio-Claudian Dynasty.

Then after nearly a century of domestic stability a civil war erupted in the summer of AD 68 and the dynasty fell. The war raged for nearly two years, and four men, Galba, Otho, Vitellius and Vespasian, were hailed emperor by the senate in the year AD 69. Vespasian, who came to power at the end of the civil war, was followed by his two sons, Titus and Domitian, which constituted the Flavian Dynasty, who ruled Rome for 27 years, from AD 69 through AD 96. The last of the "Twelve Caesars," Domitian, was murdered in a palace coup, ending the period of the "Twelve Caesars" and beginning a new era of Roman history of the adoptive emperors.

Seventeenth-century style of each of the Twelve Caesars on a square marble socle, comprising of Julius Caesar, Augustus, Tiberius, Caligula, Claudius, Nero, Galba, Otho, Vitellius, Vespasian, Titus, and Domitian. *~ credit Christie's ~*

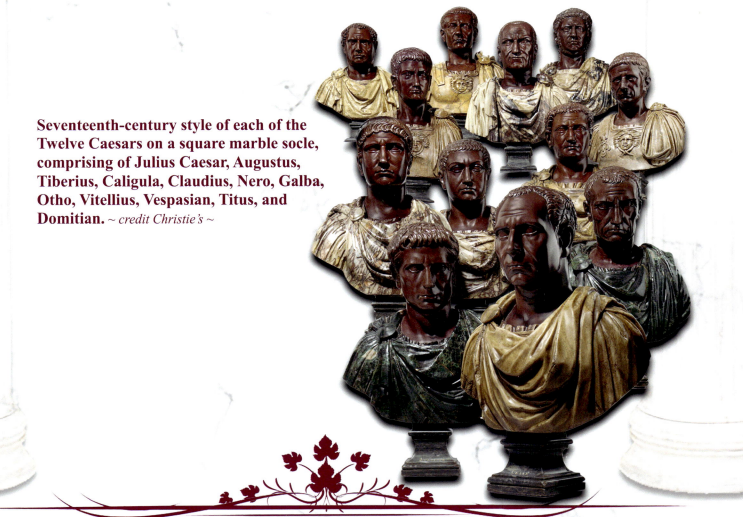

SILVER DENARII OF THE XII CAESARS

Julius Caesar Augustus Tiberius

Caligula Claudius Nero

Galba Otho Vitellius

Vespasian Titus Domitian

Titus

Rare bronze Sestertius Struck in AD 80 During the Reign of Titus
Flavian Amphitheater Obverse with Emperor Titus on the Reverse

~ COINS OF THE XII CAESARS ~

The coins of the "Twelve Caesars" are tangible tributes to Rome's emperors, struck in precious metals, that have survived many generations as living testaments of this historic era. Collecting coins of the Caesars was popularized during the Renaissance with the rediscovery of the remarkable works by ancient Roman historian and writer Suetonius, 'Lives of the Twelve Caesars.' Beginning in the 16th century, travelers to Italy began collecting coins of the Caesars, and the hobby quickly spread throughout the world.

Coins of the Twelve Caesars can be collected in copper, bronze, silver, or gold. The Gold Aureus was the economic standard of the Roman world for about four centuries, regularly struck from the 1th century BC to the beginning of the 4th century AD. The Caesar's vast conquests and military campaigns throughout the Mediterranean produced more gold for coinage and necessitated a standardized form of payment and trade. This 8-gram coin struck in nearly pure gold, became the basic gold monetary unit of ancient Rome and the Roman world.

From before the times of the Caesars, coinage was used for political propaganda and to pay tribute to rulers. Moneyers designed coins consisting of images of ancestral figures, traditional deities, and mythological scenes providing historians a window into these ancient's cultures beliefs and philosophies. In 44 BC, images of living individuals became legal to strike on coins, kicking off a long tradition of Roman rulers gracing one or both sides of the precious metal pieces. Gold Aureus coins of the Twelve Caesars features a portrait on the obverse and a symbolic design or tribute portraits on the reverse and are spectacular historical evidence of the nature of the times.

Collecting Gold Aureus of the Twelve Caesars can be one of the most desirable and challenging endeavors of numismatic collecting. Each of the 12 coins, reflect the reign of a Roman ruler from Julius Caesar to the Empire's last leader, Caesar Domitian. Building a complete set of "Twelve Caesars" is an exercise in education, patience, and perseverance, becoming a truly rewarding pursuit blending the hobby and history together.

Gold Aureus Obverse Caesar Portraits from the XII Caesars Legacy Collection

GOLD AUREI OF THE TWELVE CAESARS

Julius Caesar

Augustus

Tiberius

Caligula

Claudius

Nero

Galba

Otho

Vitellius

Vespasian

Titus

Domitian

NGC CERTIFIED OBVERSE AND REVERSE OF RARE GOLD AUREUS
FROM THE XII CAESARS LEGACY COLLECTION

~ THE ROMAN GOLD AUREUS ~

The gold coins of ancient Rome are known as "Aureus" coins. Their size is about the same as a modern-day Jefferson Nickel. In ancient Rome they were the same size as a silver denarius, a coin which was widely used in everyday commerce by average Roman citizens. The gold aureus coins were valued at 25 silver denarii and were struck infrequently before the time of Julius Caesar and were primarily used to make large payments for loyalty from captured loot of conquered territories. However, with Julius' rapid ascent to power and popularity, the coins were struck in larger quantities, and undoubtedly helped Julius Caesar amass one of the most powerful and loyal armies the world has ever known.

There is little doubt the prosperity and reach of Rome can be directly related to the large minting of gold aureus coins from the 1st century BC to the beginning of the 4th century AD. However, by the 4th century AD the aureus had undergone significant devaluations by way of the reduction of weight in gold content. It was eventually replaced by the gold solidus in the 4th century AD. Standardized weights of the aureus were established by Julius Caesar. This brilliant standardization helped create a more stable and trusted trade among the first Caesar's expanding empire. The standardized weight set by Julius Caesar was about 8 grams of more than 99% pure gold. Interestingly, as the empire declined over the next four centuries, so did the weight or real value of the gold aureus.

The weight of the aureus was decreased to 7.3 grams during the reign of Nero (r. AD 54–68). After the reign of Marcus Aurelius (r. AD 161–180) the production of aurei decreased significantly, and the weight was further decreased to 6.5 grams by the time of Caracalla (r. AD 211–217). During the third century, gold pieces were introduced in a variety of fractions and multiples, making it hard to determine the intended denomination of a gold coin. History shows us that the empire was in rapid decline and loyalties of faraway armies had eroded significantly. Due to the decline or devaluation of the gold aureus, the gold solidus was introduced by Diocletian (r. AD 284–305) around AD 301. These new gold coins of the Roman Empire weighed about 5.5 grams. However, Diocletian's solidus was struck only in small quantities, and thus had only minimal economic effect.

The solidus was reintroduced by Constantine I (r. AD 306–337) in AD 312, permanently replacing the aureus as the gold coin of the Roman Empire. The solidus was struck at a rate of 72 to a Roman pound of pure gold, each coin weighing 4.5 grams. The debasement of Rome's currencies is in large part due to the excesses of daily life and drop in productivity as an empire. It gives us a base line in history of the rise and fall of great empires such as Rome. At the time the aureus was replaced with the solidus, the empire had declined significantly and so had its currencies values. By this time, the solidus was worth 275,000 of the increasingly debased denarii. However, regardless of the size or weight of the aureus, the coin's purity was little affected. Analysis of the Roman aureus shows the purity level to be near to 24-carat gold, or more than 99%.

**Vespasian
Reign AD 69-70**

*Ch MS
Strike: 5/5
Surface: 5/5*

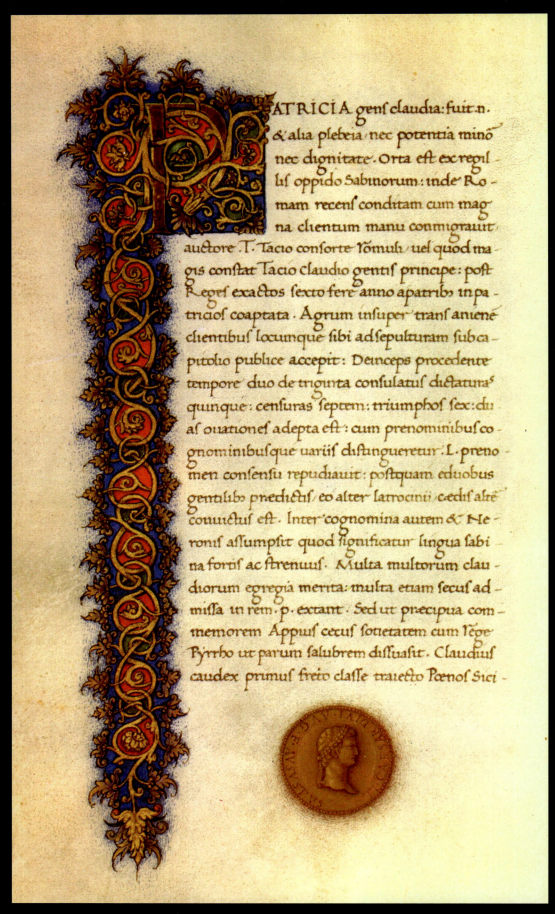

ATRICIA gens claudia: fuit .n.
& alia plebeia nec potentia mino
nec dignitate. Orta est ex regil
lis oppido Sabinorum: inde Ro
mam recens conditam cum mag
na clientum manu conmigrauit
auctore .T. Tacio consorte Romuli uel quod ma
gis constat Tacio claudio gentis principe: post
Reges exactos sexto fere anno apatrib; in pa
tricios coaptata. Agrum insuper trans aniene
clientibus locumque sibi ad sepulturam sub ca
pitolio publice accepit: Deinceps procedente
tempore duo de triginta consulatus dictaturas
quinque: censuras septem: triumphos sex: du
as ouationes adepta est: cum prenominibus co
gnominibusque uariis distingueretur. L. preno
men consensu repudiauit: postquam eduobus
gentilibus predictis; eo alter latrocinii cædis altre
conuictus est. Inter cognomina autem & Ne
ronis assumpsit quod significatur lingua sabi
na fortis ac strenuus. Multa multorum clau
diorum egregia merita: multa etiam secus ad
missa in rem. p. extant. Sed ut precipua com
memorem Appius cæcus societatem cum rege
Pyrrho ut parum salubrem dissuasit. Claudius
caudex primus freto classe traiecto Pœnos Sici

~ SUETONIUS ~

Gaius Suetonius Tranquillus, was born in the year of the Four Emperors, around AD 69. Best known for his famous work in AD 121, 'De Vita Caesarium,' which translates from Latin to "About the Life of the Caesars." This set of biographies begins with Julius Caesar in 44 BC all the way through the last of the Flavian Dynasty in AD 96 and is considered by Roman historians as his most important work. 'The Twelve Caesars,' was considered very significant in antiquity and remains a primary source on Roman history today.

The "Twelve Caesars" is a collective biography of the Roman Empire's first leaders, Julius Caesar, Augustus, Tiberius, Caligula, Claudius, Nero, Galba, Otho, Vitellius, Vespasian, Titus, and Domitian. The work tells the tale of each Caesar's life according to a set formula: the descriptions of appearance, omens, family history, quotes, and then a history is given in a consistent order for each Caesar. His works are largely responsible for a vivid picture of Roman society and its leaders, morally and politically decadent, that gave the world an inside view of the "Twelve Caesars."

Suetonius' style by some is considered as more of tabloid journalism, 2,000 years ahead of its time. He was well placed to pick up gossip, as his father commanded a legion for Otho in AD 69 and he entered the imperial civil service, giving him access to imperial libraries and archives. With a position close to the imperial court he was able to access otherwise private sources for his work, and he certainly did not hold back on revealing the sometimes-sordid details of Rome's most famously debauched emperors. Suetonius was free from the bias of the senatorial class that distorts much Roman historical writing. So, he was open with scandalous gossip, but largely silent on the growth, administration, and defense of the empire.

His sketches of the habits and appearance of the emperors are invaluable, using "characteristic anecdotes" through twelve detailed enduring portraits, drawn with skill to differentiate each Caesar by stressing their most prominent characteristics. Suetonius offered more than entertainment, he was objective and nonjudgmental, where other great historians like Tacitus, were biased and censorious. Suetonius wrote with firmness and brevity, using exact, appropriate words and skilled vocabulary, enhanced his pictorial vividness, to bring the Twelve Caesars alive. Above all he was unrhetorical, unpretentious, and capable of molding complex events into lucid expressions of history

For those who wish to truly understand Roman life, particularly the personal lives of its leaders, Suetonius' book is a must addition to your library. No one who truly admires Roman history can proclaim so without reading this fun and historical view of the world we call ancient Rome.

Lo storico Svetonio aveva raccolte nella sua casa una collezione di anticaglie.

Gaius Suetonius Tranquillus Roman Historian and Biographer
~ Public Domain ~

Twelve Caesars Portraits

Etchings were Copied by Flemish Engravers
in the Late 16th and Early 17th Centuries

~ XII CAESARS PORTRAITS ~

The Caesars series of half-length portraits of Roman emperors in this book, were originally painted by Titian between AD 1536-1540 for Federico II, Duke of Mantua, inspired by the book 'Lives of the Twelve Caesars,' authored by the ancient Roman writer Suetonius, an historic set of twelve biographies of Julius Caesar and the first 11 emperors of the Roman Empire. The first eleven paintings were created by Titian, with the twelfth portrait added by Giulio Romano. Rome's emperors were depicted in classical poses, wearing armor, and flowing draped clothing, accompanied by various objects such as swords and staffs.

The Twelve Caesars portraits were copied by Bernardino Campi in AD 1561 for Francesco Ferdinando d'Ávalos, governor of Milan. Thankfully, the portraits were copied by Flemish engravers in the late 16th and early 17th centuries. In AD 1628, the paintings were sold to Charles I of England, then passed into the collection of Philip IV of Spain in AD 1651, after the beheading execution of Charles I in 1649 by the English Commonwealth. The paintings were all destroyed in a catastrophic fire at the Royal Alcazar of Madrid in AD 1734 so now only copies and engravings exist of the legendary Twelve Caesars Portraits.

**Self-Portrait of Tiziano Vecellio
Known as Titian (c. AD 1490-1576)**
~ Public Domain ~

**Bernardino Campi Self-Portrait
Painting a Portrait of a Woman**
~ Public Domain ~

**Portrait of Julius Caesar
by Follower of Bernardino Campi**
~ credit Sotheby's ~

CAIUS JULIUS CÆSAR, DICT: PERPET:

Julius Cæsar, was born in 654ᵗʰ Year of the City of Rome, on the 12 day of the month Quinctilis, afterward from him named July. He obtain'd
the place of Great Pontiff, when very young. In the City year 694. he enter'd into a Conspiracy with Pompey and Crassus, That nothing should
be done in the Common Wealth which displeased any of them. This was called the first Triumvirate, and lasted about 16 years. In the first Consulship of
Cæsar, he suffered Tully to be banished by Clodius, The Temple of Jerusalem was rifled by Crassus in one of his Expeditions, which prov'd his last. Crassus
being slain, soon after, a Civil war arose, between Cæsar and Pompey. At Pharsalia in Greece, Pompeys Army was routed, and he killed in Egypt. After
this Cæsar carried on his Conquests till he became Absolute, and was made PERPETUAL DICTATOR. He is truly stil'd first EMPEROUR of Rome, tho'
when he was called King, he would seem to discountenance it by saying, That he was not King but Cæsar. He was artfull and bold in Councils, and in management.
He would write, and dictate to several Secretaries at the same time. He was very successfull in War, gaining forty nine Battles, in fifty, which he fought. His
clemency sometimes to the Conquered, and his Bounty to his Soldiers, gain'd him great Glory, as well as his unparall'd Victories. When he was General of
the Roman Forces in Gallia, he invaded this Island of Brittain. He wrote a Book of his own Actions and expeditions, which is called his Commentaries.
Four times he was Created Consul, and five, he entered Rome in Triumph. His Vices were scandalous and notorious, in the midst of all his Honours. He
was so exceedingly addicted to Women, that besides his Intrigues with Cleopatra, and others abroad, He was infamous in Rome it self, for debauching one
of Cato's Aunts, and perswading her also to prostitute her Daughter to him. His Ambition was so great as to prove his own Ruin at last, when it had first destroyed Millions of Lives and Families. Tho in the general, he cannot but be admired, as M.ʳ Bayle observes, yet when one considers the prodigious number
of men whose Death, Poverty, or Slavery, he occasion'd, one can hardly forbear abhorring him. After many warnings of his Death, he was murdered in the
Senate House, by Brutus, Cassius, and other Conspirators; receiveing in his Body Twenty three wounds. A remarkable vengeance was however observed to pursue, & cut
off those Murderers.

~ JULIUS CAESAR ~

Julius Caesar needs no introduction to those familiar with the foundations of western civilization. Even among the great figures of the ancient world, Julius Caesar has few equals. As a self-proclaimed "Dictator for Life," he had ideas well ahead of his time, and much of what he did and did not do is the foundation for the way societies are run to this day. He rose to power quickly and extended the reach of the Roman world and the rise of an Empire. At a time when armies were paid primarily in gold and land, he amassed one of the most loyal and successful armies the world had ever seen.

His legions are legendary for their loyalty and are responsible for stretching the influence of the Empire. They were the first Romans to step foot on what we know today as Great Britain. They conquered Gaul which made him immensely popular throughout the Empire. His "Crossing of the Rubicon" and return to Rome was considered treasonous by many in power. A civil war ensued in which Julius Caesar's legions were able to crush any resistance from the Roman Senate to his absolute rule of the emergent Roman Empire.

Some within the Senate feared his popularity would eventually make him too powerful for them to control. Fearing for the good of Rome, a plot was hatched by a group of angry senators, led by Cassius and Brutus, to assassinate Julius. The plot was famously successful on the "Ides of March" - March 15, 44 BC. Civil war was again fueled, and the rulers who followed Julius Caesar forever shaped the course of Rome and western civilization as we know it. Julius Caesar was the first Roman emperor to be deified as a God, and the last ruler of the Roman Republic. The King of Diamonds in a deck of playing cards symbolizes him, and the month of July is also named for him.

He created the standardized Gold Aureus coin, weighing 8 grams, hand struck in 99% pure gold, and minted in large quantities to expand his empire and fuel commerce. Julius Caesar's fame and accomplishments make his gold coins always in high demand and extremely difficult to find. Owning one of these coins is one of the most prestigious accomplishments for collectors of numismatic history.

TWELVE CAESARS

Julius Caesar, d.44 BC
AV Aureus (8.06g)
c.46 BC A.Hirtius praetor
obv Pietas. rv implements

3987321-002

MS★
Strike: 5/5
Surface: 4/5

NGC
ANCIENTS

MINT STATE STAR • STRIKE: 5/5 • SURFACE: 4/5

World Famous Dictator of the Roman Republic

Julius Caesar is one of the greatest figures in human history. He amassed one of the most successful and loyal armies in the world, and extended Rome's reach dramatically. He rose to power quickly and his political story is one of the most well-known in history, making his coins some of the most popular and most desired coins in the world.

It is amazing that specimens still exist in this condition to this day, a testament to how long they have been collected and cherished. With the vast number of museums dedicated to Roman Culture and the history of the world, no matter the condition, a Julius Caesar Aureus will always garner interest, but in Mint State Star condition, it is a must have key piece for every collector of the Twelve Caesars.

With an excellent strike (5/5) and nearly flawless surfaces (4/5) this Julius Caesar Aureus is spectacular. It is simply jaw dropping. The sheer history alone that this coin possesses is enough to stimulate the minds of any astute historian. Take into consideration how it is possible that this coin is still in Mint State condition after all this time and it is quite remarkable. It is impossible to gaze upon its gracious surfaces and not be enamored by the elegant simplicity and bold details of every surface. It is truly a masterpiece.

II. D. OCT. AUGUSTUS.

OCTAVIUS was the adopted Heir of Julius Cæsar, being the Son of his Sisters Daughter. He was born when Cicero was Consul, and gained the Consulship for himself before he was 20 years old. Being disobliged by the Senate, he agrees with Anthony, and Lepidus who make the Second Triumvirate. Brutus and Caßius were Conquer'd at Philippi, and kill themselves, some say with the same Weapons that they us'd to stab Cæsar. Sextus Pompeius was also routed and kill'd. After this, Augustus subduing his Partners in the Triumvirate, he became Absolute and from ye Conquest of Anthony, at the Battle of Actium, began a new Æra of Time. Vipanius Agrippa would then have persuaded him to lay down his Power, but he was disswaded by Mecænas. Thereupon he reform'd the Senate, had the Title of AUGUSTUS given him, and from that time exceedingly won the Peoples Hearts. He detected several Treasons, and Conquering Cinna by kindneß, had no more Conspiracies form'd against him. He shut the Temple of Janus, in token of Universal Peace, and taxed the World. And then was born ye great SAVIOUR of Mankind, our LORD JESUS CHRIST. About 4 years after his birth, ye Temple of Janus was opened again. Tiberius was then adopted, and Conquer'd much, & having finish'd ye German Wars obtain'd a Share in the Empire with Augustus. Who having made his Will, & number'd ye Citizens of Rome, (4,173,000) and left in writing an account of ye Empire, as also Directions to his Succeßor, he died at Nola, in ye Arms of his Wife Livia. He reign'd from ye Battle of Actium 44 years, and from ye full Establishment of his Authorite by ye Senate 41 years. The principal Vices of Augustus, were, his Cruel and Fallacious Actions during ye Triumvirate, and his Love of Women. But his innumerable Acts of Wisdom, and Virtue, make his Faults generally overlook'd. His motto was Festina lente: which he explain'd by saying, That is done speedily Enough, that is done well Enough. In Augustus's time, Cicero was beheaded by Anthony's procurement; Julia was banished for her Lewdneß; Herod maßacred ye Infants at Bethlehem; Ovid ye Poet was banished for his loose amorous Poems & John yt Harbinger of divine love was born. Archelaus was banished, & his Dominion reduced to a Roman Province. And Judas of Galilee arose and form'd a new Sect.

~ AUGUSTUS ~

Rome's first emperor, Augustus, was one of the most successful rulers of the ancient world and considered the founder of the Roman Empire. Born Caius Octavius, he took the name Caesar Octavianus when he was adopted by his great-uncle Julius Caesar, who was impressed with his characteristics, and made Octavian his heir.

After Caesars assassination, Octavian used Caesar's fortune and political alliances to seize control of the Roman Empire, defeating Caesar's enemies in war, including former ally Mark Antony as well as his lover, Queen Cleopatra VII of Egypt. He emerged victorious in a civil war that had raged for decades. He was given the title 'Augustus' from the senate after bringing peace and prosperity to the Greco-Roman world. After consolidating power, he artfully transformed the Roman government from a fallen republic into a monarchy.

Augustus did not claim dictatorial powers, unlike his late great-uncle Julius. He asked only for the power of a tribune, which would provide him veto power over legislation, and proconsular or military authority over provinces with sizeable armies. With these powers, Augustus improved the city of Rome, particularly as a reformer who streamlined the government and tried to impose moral change. Augustus ruled the Mediterranean world and had the longest reign of 41 years, starting from 27 BC to AD 14. Augustus was a leader who, despite his power, avoided being perceived as a monarch. Remarkably he lived until the age of 75 and upon his death he was widely mourned by the citizens of Rome. Much of his political and social legacy live to this day and the month of August is named after him.

The coins of his empire are routinely collected and summarily very hard to find. Although he lived to the ripe old age of 75, his coin portrait remained youthful and idealized. Many design types were produced under his reign and struck in abundance, inspiring collectors to make an attempt to collect them all. Incredibly, few have survived in high grade.

II • AUGUSTUS AUREUS

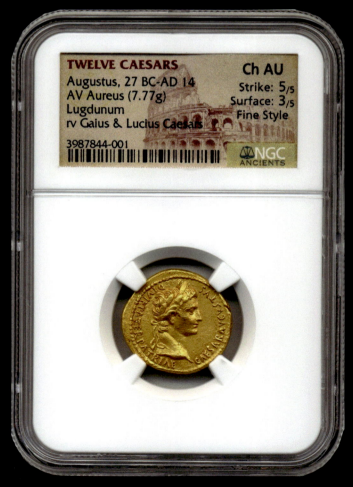

CHOICE AU • STRIKE: 5/5 • SURFACE: 3/5
~ FINE STYLE ~

The Founder of the Roman Empire, and its First Emperor

"Have I played the part well? Then, applaud as I exit."

Such were the last words of Emperor Augustus as he lay dying in AD 14 after ruling over one of the most peaceful and stable periods in Roman history compared with the previous period of civil war after the assassination of his maternal great-uncle, Julius Caesar.

Many consider Augustus to be the greatest ruler of the Roman Empire and the most influential of the 12 Caesars. His 41-year tenure as Caesar brought stability and put the building blocks in place for its continued expansion and success. He plays a pivotal role in the culture of Rome as well as the expectations of its future citizens. His influence was felt across multiple generations.

His productive reign was marked by an expansion of the Roman Empire and strengthening of its political infrastructure. He developed several important public works, including a standing army, a police force, a courier system, a fire department, and an improved network of roads.

With only 2 finer at NGC, this Augustus Aureus is a tremendous example of an amazing leader. The portrait is a perfect personification of his long reigning tenure, and the honoring of his grandsons on the reverse is a nod to the future of Rome.

III. TIBERIUS CÆSAR.

TIBERIUS *having been adopted by* Augustus, *and affociated with him in the Empire, he was defired to take the Government wholly upon himself, after* Augustus's *Death. He adopted* Germanicus, *and pretended great Friendship for him; but being Envious at his Succeffes, and his Univerfal Efteem among the People, by the directions and councels of* Tiberius*, that brave and moft accomplifht man was poyfon'd. His Death was after reveng'd upon* Piso*.* Tiberius *advances his Son* Drufus *to the Tribunitian Power, who is poyson'd by* Sejanus's *procurement, having firft Seduc'd and debaucht his wife. After the Death of* Drufus*,* Tiberius *became monftroufly Cruel and Tyrannical: And retiring from* Rome *to* Caprea*, he gave up himself to all manner of Lewdnefs, and Lecheries too Shameful to mention. He was a Drunkard so remarkable, that he would be called by a nick name to shew he made it his Boast. But he had fuch Remorse, and fufpicious fears, an horrible Confufions in his own mind, that he once writ to the Senate, confeffing to them, That the* GODS *had fo afflicted and Confounded him, He knew no how or what to write.* Tacitus *fays, if one could look into fuch a Beaft, He might fee the marks of thousand Stripes and ftabs. But notwithftanding these, has wickednefs encreas'd, and rag'd moft Violently, when Age and nature should have led to correct it. He was univerfally abhor'd, and being perfon or fuffer'd to Death (as Authors differently write)* Rome *was filld with joy, and the common Cry was, Throw* Tiberius *into the* Tiber*. Others threatned to drag his Pale Carcafe into the Place for common Malefactors. He reigned 23 years, 7 months and some odd Days. In this Reign the Amphitheatre at* Fidenæ *fell, and killed 20,000 peple, and wounded 30,000 more. The whole family of* Sejanus *was deftroy'd for his wickednefs.* Pilate *was made Governor of* Judea*, the power of Life and Death was taken from the Jews. S. John Baptist appeared in the Spirit of* Elias *as the forerunner of the Meffias.* JESUS CHRIST *preached Salvation, and wrought innumerable miracles, and lived a moft holy Life, was Crucified, and rose from the dead, and ascended to Heaven, and sent the Holy Ghoft.* Tiberius *propofed to the Senate that* JESUS *should be numbred among their* GOD'S*. A Phœnix is faid to appear about the end of this Reign.*

~ TIBERIUS ~

Tiberius was born into an ancient Roman aristocratic family. His father fell on the wrong side of the civil wars and so Tiberius began his life as a fugitive. However, his fortunes changed when his mother Livia divorced his father and married Augustus. Tiberius was an extraordinary general and went on to have a promising military career. Tiberius' service to Rome was second only to that of Augustus. He was forced to divorce his wife Vipsania so he could marry Augustus's widowed daughter Julia but ended up unhappily married to her. Augustus disliked Tiberius but adopted him as his heir. Tiberius was neither the first choice of Augustus nor popular with the Roman people, but Augustus reluctantly had Tiberius succeed him to the imperial office because he deemed no one else suitable.

As emperor, Tiberius initially ruled with conservative modesty and discretion, reluctant to act against critics. He was beset with troubles that stemmed primarily from dynastic infighting. His reign became so difficult that he abandoned the capital and spent his last decade ruling in relative isolation on the island of Capri. Tiberius was under the influence of General Sejanus, the head of the Praetorian Guard, and became more brutal, tyrannical, and sexually deviant, seemingly reveling in who he truly was. Meanwhile, in faraway Judaea, the Roman Procurator Pontius Pilate crucified Jesus Christ.

His chief fault was the severity he showed to senators suspected of disloyalty, and this has led to his being harshly treated by history. In later years, Tiberius's debaucheries and his preoccupation with his own sensual pleasures are infamous. Tiberius died hating himself and was despised by the people of Rome, who greeted the news of his death at age 77 with joy and jubilation. At his death, he left the Roman Empire prosperous and stable, he also left the imperial office to his grand-nephew and adopted grandson, the notorious Gaius "Caligula."

Demand for Tiberius coins is fueled by his notoriety as an emperor, as well as his reign during the time of Christ. The coinage of Tiberius is relatively common and standardized compared to the hundreds of different types of Augustus coinage. The obverse bore an idealized portrait, and the reverse depicted a seated female figure, identified as Tiberius's mother, Livia who lived to the extraordinary age of 87. Ironically, the denarius of Tiberius was destined to become one of the most famous ancient coins for reasons having nothing to do with the emperor. Biblical scholars consider it to be the famous "Tribute Penny" from the Book of Mark in the Bible. The tribute penny was the coin that was shown to Jesus when he made his famous speech "Render unto Caesar."

Ruler in the Time of Christ and His Crucifixion

Tiberius, the stepson of Augustus was known as a dark and reclusive ruler. He reigned during the time of Christ's crucifixion and he is known for his conservative growth of the Empire, generally avoiding smaller military confrontations with neighboring tyrants.

The coinage of Tiberius is synonymous with the Bible, as it is believed by biblical scholars that his silver denarius was referenced in Matthew 22:15-22 (NIV) "Then the Pharisees went out and laid plans to trap Him in his words. They sent their disciples to Him along with the Herodians. "Teacher, we know you are a man of integrity and that you teach the way of God and truth. You are not swayed by others, because you pay no attention to who they are. Tell us then, what is your opinion? Is it right to pay the imperial tax to Caesar or not?"

Jesus replied, knowing their evil intent, "You hypocrites, why are you trying trap me? Show me the coin used for paying the tax." They brought him a silver denarius, and he asked them, "Whose image is this? And whose inscription?"

"Caesar's", they replied. Then he said to them, "so give back to Caesar what is Caesar's…".
In AD 37 Tiberius fell ill and at word that he was not dying fast enough, it is believed by some that he was finished off by Caligula. Romans reportedly rejoiced at the news of his death.

Minted in Lugdunum (modern day Lyon), the gold aurei of Tiberius are common in lower grade and extremely scarce in Mint State. The specimen here exhibits a perfect strike and typical surface grades, with superb overall eye appeal. It draws you in with deeply lustrous fields and crisp detail. The obverse features the laureate head of Tiberius facing right, and the reverse features Livia, the wife of his adopted father Augustus, depicted as the goddess of Peace.

IV. C CÆSAR CALIGULA.

CALIGULA *was the Son of Germanicus by Agrippina, and Nephew to Tiberius. He took his name from the military Dress in which he chose to appear. At his being made Emperour, his People were transported with an excess of Joy, and express'd a most extravagant Affection for him. They thought nothing too great or good to expect from the Son of the Universally belov'd Germanicus. But they were soon punish'd for their idolizing this Prince; after he had reigned well for about 8 months, he became one of the most tyrannical and brutish creatures that ever liv'd. He wish'd for uncommon Disasters to make his Reign memorable. He was so impious as to build and dedicate a Temple to his own Divinity, and plaid such Pranks in Religion as plainly shew he was disorder'd in his head. His murders, and Executions, were innumerable. He wish'd the Roman People had but one Neck, that he might dispatch them all at a Blow. At some times his Covetousness prevailed, so that he would amass together vast sums of mony, and roul himself upon it as his greatest Recreation. At other times his Prodigality was so amazing, that he would quite drain his Exchequer: it was the case when he built a Bridge over the Sea 3 miles and a half in length, and undertook his Expedition with a large Army, upon a perfect Don Quixott Errand. After these Extravagancies follow'd all manner of Rapines, Cruelties, and flatteries to replenish his Coffers. He was Excessively and Unnaturally Lustfull: scarce any Lady of Beauty or quality escap'd his Leudness. He Committed Incest with his 3 natural Sisters; and then prostituted two of them to his Vile Companions, banish'd them. The Punishment of his Vices follows. He was so terrified at a Clap of Thunder that he would hide himself under a Bed. All the Love his People bare to him at first, turn'd into a violent hatred at last. Chærea, one of his officers Stab'd him, as he was Passing from his Palace to his Baths, with this expression, Tyrant think upon this. At the same time he received thirty Wounds from others. The Vengeance of Heaven fell upon his Family also. And his very Coin was ordered to be melted down by the Senate, that no mark or feature of him might remain to common view. He reigned but 3 years, 10 months, and 8 days, being cut off in the 29 year of his Age. In this Short Reign the APOSTLES of our LORD JESUS CHRIST went about preaching Repentance and Salvation to a Considerable part of the world. St. Matthew wrote his Gospel. Herod and Herodias were banish'd. Pilate kill'd himself. Cornelius became the first Christian Convert among the Gentiles.*

~ CALIGULA ~

Few emperors are as infamous as Caligula, whose sordid reputation still precedes him nearly 2,000 years after his reign. Born as 'Caius', or Gaius on August 31st in the year AD 12, he is better known as 'Caligula', or Little Boots, the nickname given him by the soldiers of his father Germanicus. His father was a successful and very popular general, and the nephew of Emperor Tiberius. Caligula's mother, Agrippina the Elder, who was Augustus' granddaughter, is remembered in history as a paragon of womanly virtue.

As a boy Caligula would often entertain his father's legionaries by dressing in miniature Roman battle gear and 'drill' the troops. As a young man, Caligula would show exaggerated affection to those in power but acted cruelly to everyone else. The deaths of his father, mother, and two elder brothers left Caius Caligula as his great-uncle Tiberius' heir.

When he became emperor, Caligula was jubilantly received, since Tiberius was so hated, and Germanicus was so loved by the people. At first, he made a good start as emperor, funding several public games and new buildings, but became severely ill seven months after his accession. The optimism of Caligula's fellow citizens was replaced by grave disappointment, when he embarked on a career of cruelty and caprice, before descending into a "monster."

Caligula most likely suffered from a form of insanity and became increasingly irrational with the passage of time. He ruthlessly persecuted members of the Senate, committed incest with his three sisters, and demanded sexual intercourse from respectable married women of Rome. He believed he was a living god, and the Senators were unable to otherwise check their emperor's absolute powers, when several plotted his murder. His reign of terror ended when Caligula, his wife Caesonia, and his daughter Drusilla were killed by assassins led by a Captain of the Praetorian Guard, as well as several senators, in a palace coup in AD 41.

Caligula fires the popular imagination far more than many other emperors with similarly short stints on the throne. His given name–Gaius (or Caius) Julius Caesar Germanicus–appears on his coinage, variously abbreviated. His silver and gold coins are exceedingly rare in any condition and are always in high demand. The coins of Caligula are usually the most difficult to locate when completing a set of the Twelve Caesars. The rare availability of Caligula coins can sometimes make it a stumbling block for collectors. They are challenging to attain for even the most advanced collector, and when found, they become the cornerstone coin to any 12-piece set of Gold Caesars.

TWELVE CAESARS
Caligula, AD 37-41
AV Aureus (7.90g)
rv radiate hd. of Augustus
or Tiberius betw. stars
3990551-001

AU
Strike: 5/5
Surface: 4/5

NGC
ANCIENTS

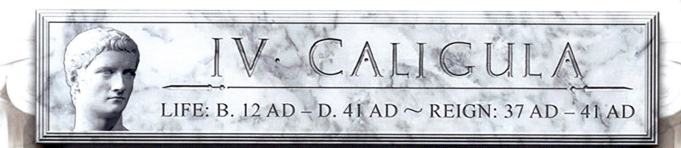
An Unquenchable Thirst for Power
Self-Proclaimed Living God

Caligula was the great nephew of Tiberius and is believed by some to have finished off Tiberius while he was on his deathbed, although it is often refuted that he could not follow through with it. The first six months of his reign started uneventful and moderate, but his ego quickly took hold and an unquenchable thirst for power and excessive personal pleasures ensued. Although claiming oneself as a god was generally frowned upon by anyone in power, Caligula became so infatuated with himself that he forced many to worship him as a living god. He was ultimately assassinated by the Praetorian Guard and a group of Senators.

Tied for the Finest Known graded by NGC, this particular design type is fascinating for the continued debate as to the features on the reverse. Some argue that it is Tiberius, a nod to the previous emperor, and Caligula's adoptive uncle. A depiction of Tiberius is a showing of continuity in the nation and a direct reflection of continued success. Others would argue that the reverse is a depiction of Augustus, honoring Caligula's great grandfather and bringing newfound glory to the Empire. Either interpretation just further heightens Caligula's perceived power over the people and boosts his ego to new heights.

Undoubtedly a power piece, this coin is a must own for every serious collector. Discovering a Caligula Aureus is a grueling task and finding one in this condition is nearly impossible.

V. D. CLAUDIUS CÆSAR

DRUSUS CLAUDIUS *was the Uncle of Caligula, and Brother of Germanicus; who till 50 years of Age liud in obscurity, Spending much of his time in Study and writing. He was chosen Emperor by the Soldiers contrary to the Determinations of the Senate; but was afterward allowed and Received by them through their Terror of the Army. This Claudius was of a ponderfull Stupid and Cowardly nature; and averse to Action any further then he was put upon it by other about him. While he was acted by the Authority of the Senate, and with the Advice of the Consuls, he did many Excellent things. He heard Caules and administred Iustice in Person. Some Brittons Coming to Seek the Protection of the Romans, being harass'd with Ciuil Wars among themselves Claudius came into this Iland; in which he manage'd so well, that there was A Temple and an Altar erected to him, and upon his return to Rome triumphal Ornaments were prepared for him. But after this, being abandon'd to Gluttony and Lust, he became Strangely forgetfull of every thing; and was So Stupidly Cruel, that he would See the most exquisite Torments inflicted on men, without any manner of Concern. He put death 35 Senators, and above 300 Equites in his reign. He was a Shamefull Property to the Lust and Politicks of his Wives; by one of which he was Sent out of the world. She first put Poyson into a Dish of Mushrooms; but being Sick and casting them up as Soon as he had eaten them, his Wife feared She had not done the Business Effectually, and therefore Sent for her Physician who on pretence of helping him to Vomit (as was usual with him after his gluttonous Excesses) put a Poysond Feather down his Throat. This he ended his Life after he had reigned 13 years 8 months, and about 20 days. In this Reign was a dreadfull Famine foretold by Agabus. Seneca was recall'd from banishment and made Tutor to Nero, who adopted by Claudius and married to his Daughter Octavia. PAUL became very famous for his Labours, Suffering, and Trauels in propagating the Faith of CHRIST. They that received it were first called CHRISTIANS, at Antioch. St Mark wrote his Gospel. St James the great was beheaded, Theudas the Impostor was defeated, 20,000 Iews were Slain in a Sedition under Cumanus Governour of Iudæa. The Virgin mary dies, And St Philip the Apostle is martyrd.*

~ CLAUDIUS ~

Claudius was born into the Julio-Claudian dynasty in 10 BC. He was the grandson of Mark Antony, brother of Germanicus, and uncle of Caligula. He was born with a physical disability which made him an embarrassment to the imperial family. In his youth, he suffered from ill health, clumsiness of manner, and coarseness of taste. The decision was made to exclude him from public life, and he became something of a domestic buffoon. Claudius was denied any military or political responsibilities even though he was the nephew of Tiberius and great-nephew of Augustus. Being ostracized earlier in his life may have protected him when purges of officials swept through the reigns of Tiberius and Caligula. He devoted himself to scholarly work, especially history. It was not until the reign of Caligula that Claudius was granted any political offices at the age of 46 years old.

When Caligula was murdered, the Praetorian Guards found 'Uncle Claudius' hiding behind a curtain expecting to be murdered too. Instead, he was dragged out and declared emperor on the spot. At 51 years old, he suffered from a variety of maladies; he was regarded as not too bright, he was slightly deaf, had fits and epileptic seizures, a funny limp, as well as several personal habits like a bad stutter and excessive drooling when overexcited.

Being the last surviving male of the Imperial family, he was made emperor and Claudius was a surprisingly effective and scrupulous leader over the next 13 years, ruling with care, attention, and skill. He was interested in public works; aqueducts in Rome, roads in the provinces, a harbor at Ostia, strengthening Rome's grain supply, and hearing judicial cases personally. History suggests that he was a bit cowardly and unreliable when it came to legal judgments. Claudius's conquest of Britain was the most significant expansion of Roman territory since Julius Caesar's invasion of Gaul. However, Claudius's relationship with the senatorial aristocracy was troubled, and he married unwisely several times.

Messalina, his much-younger third wife, had numerous affairs, and was executed for marrying her lover and trying to make him emperor when Claudius was absent from Rome. He then married his own niece, Agrippina the Younger, and favored her son Nero from another father, as his successor over his own son, Britannicus. When Agrippina suspected that Claudius was about to turn on her, she poisoned him with a dish of poisoned mushrooms, paving the way for her son, Nero to become emperor in AD 54. The following year, Claudius' son Britannicus died unnaturally.

His personal and moral failings aside, most modern historians agree that Claudius generally ruled well, and was the great expander of the Roman Empire. Much like Caligula, the coins of Claudius are always in demand. His silver and gold coins are rare and hard to find, so most buyers seek portrait bronzes for their collection. His coins were very popular with his troops at the time and circulated throughout the empire, reaching far beyond the borders of Rome.

V · CLAUDIUS

TWELVE CAESARS
Claudius, AD 41-54
AV Aureus (7.78g)
rv SPQR PP OB C S
in oak wreath
3990575-001

Ch MS
Strike: 5/5
Surface: 5/5

NGC
ANCIENTS

CHOICE MS · STRIKE: 5/5 · SURFACE: 5/5

The First Roman Emperor Born Outside of Italy (Lugdunum)

SPQR - PP - OBCS (The Senate and the Roman People - Father of the Nation - For Having Saved the Citizens)

Claudius, the fifth of the Twelve Caesars, was uncle to Caligula and is well thought to have been involved in a broad conspiracy to murder Caligula since he left the scene of the crime just before it began. After successfully seizing power he began the orchestration of the largest expansion of the Empire since the time of Augustus and began the conquest of the British Isles.

Historical accounts depict him as a well-rounded emperor. His public works, military efforts, and presence at public trials trump the accounts of some historians of the bloodthirsty and cruel Gladiator patron. Ambiguity about his death remains, and there is a debate among historians; some believe he was poisoned while others believe he died of old age.

The magnificent specimen represented before you is the Finest Known Claudius Aureus at NGC. It is breathtaking, a stunning example of detailed craftsmanship paired with artistic decadence. The fields of this coin are immaculate, and the portrait is sturdy and rugged. You can see the stern gaze and imagine the man who stood before the world, a man who was considered a father of the nation, who had been deemed a savior of the citizens and the Senate. This coin is commemorating Claudius and his achievements, it was created in his honor and stands alone as his crowning glory.

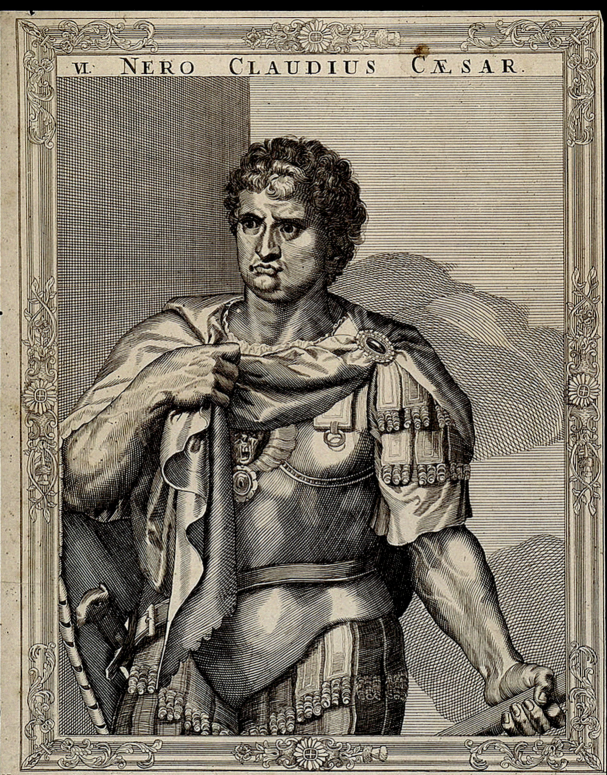

VI. NERO CLAUDIUS CÆSAR.

NERO *was so called, from a Sabin Word, that signifies* Strength *and* Fortitude. *He was the Son of* C. Domitius Ænobarbus, *by* Agrippina. *This Emperor had two Excellent Governours, Viz.* Seneca, *and* Burrhus. *At first his Government he was applauded, being perswaded to follow y.e Example of* Augustus. *But he soon began to degenerate; and falling out with his mother, upon which he was afraid she should make a Party, to set up* Britannicus, *(the Son of* Claudius Cæsar *by a former Wife)* Nero *first poysons* Britannicus, *and then orders his Mother to be murder'd; some say after he had incestuously defil'd her. He deflower'd the Vestals; slew his Sister,* Antonia; *murdered his Aunt,* (Domitia) *and his son in Law,* (Rufinus) *and his true wives* (Octavia *and* Poppæa *some say he poyson'd* Burrhus *his Gouernour, as he was also the Death of* Seneca *his famous Tutor, and of the great Poet* Lucan, *and the polite* Petronius; *with others not to be number'd. He fir'd the City of* Rome, *and then charg'd the innocent Christians with it, persecuting and tormenting them for it. His Punishment for these monstrous Crimes was very signal. He had such Horrors of mind that he complain'd of being tormented by the Infernal Furies. He was haunted with most dreadfull apprehensions of Ghosts, particularly his murder'd Mothers. He was distracted with repeated Accounts of Insurrections; but at the same time infatuated with his Pleasures & Musical Instruments, so that he went on doting about these to the very moment of his Destruction. He was at last abandon'd of All his Friends and adjudg'd by the Senate to an infamous Death, to avoid which, he became his own Executioner. He died horribly, not Expiring till some time after he had run himself upon his Dagger. He reigned 13 years 7 months, and about 29 days. In this Reign, S.t Peter is suppos'd to go to* Babylon. Cerinthus *began his Heresie. The Jews were deluded by an Ægyptian. S.t* PAUL *goes to* Ephesus; *travel'd into* Europe; *returns to* Jerusalem; *is seiz'd there, and tried for his Life; appeals to* Cæsar, *and is sent to* Rome; *writes his Canonical Epistles from several places, and makes a multitude of Conveys, goes thro innumerable Labours and Hardships, and at last was beheaded. In this reign also S.t* Luke *wrote his Gospel, and his Acts of the Apostles. S.t* Matthew *and S.t* Mark *died. S.t* James *was martyr'd at* Jerusalem, Matthias *was chosen. The first* GENERAL PERSECUTION *was raised. S.t* Andrew *and S.t* Peter *were Crucified. The Jews were horribly massacred at* Cæsarea *and* Alexandria. Jerusalem *was invested, and the Christians fled to* Pella.

~ NERO ~

When you think of Roman Emperor Nero, you probably imagine him fiddling on the roof while Rome burned, which is a myth. However, the notorious Nero was responsible for some of the worst debauchery, decadence, and violence the Roman Empire ever produced.

Born Lucius Domitius Ahenobarbus in AD 37 in Antium, his paternal family, the Domitians, were aristocrats with a long history and a poor reputation. His father died when he was just three, and his mother, Caligula's sister Agrippina the Younger, married the Emperor Claudius. As the adopted son and successor of his stepfather Claudius, Lucius' ambitions were restricted to competing in musical and dramatic contests, receiving many honors as a leading youth in the Trojan Games. His name was changed to Nero Claudius Caesar which was given due to his lineage from Augustus.

He came to power in AD 54 at only 17 years old, after the poisoning death of his stepfather, Claudius, allegedly by his mother Agrippina, who was ambitious, ruthless, and determined that her son should be emperor. Weak, shallow, and vain, Nero demonstrated how badly hereditary monarchy can work when applied to the Roman empire's absolute autocracy. He quickly shed the influence of his mother by ordering her murder, and subsequently murdered his aunt, his ex-wife, and a half-brother who had claim to the throne.

Nero ruled Rome from AD 54 to AD 68, and first vowed to reign in a more open, less corrupt way than his predecessors. While Nero carried out some reforms, he was more interested in public games and theatrical and musical performances. He reigned with little tolerance or attention to the annoying details of running an empire. As one of the most notorious emperors of Rome, Nero is known for executing anyone who did not agree with him or he felt was a threat to his power. Considered by many to be the Antichrist, he rounded up Christians and killed them in horrible, sadistic ways, making their deaths as painful and unpleasant as possible. Nero's eccentricities continued in the tradition of his predecessors in mental and personal perversions. Eventually, his bad behavior caught up with him, and Nero was declared a public enemy by the senate and fled for his life. With nowhere to run, he committed suicide with the help of one of his aides. Nero was a narcissist to the bitter end as legend has his dying words reported to be, "What an artist dies in me!" After a reign of nearly 14 years, Nero was the last of the Julio-Claudians to reign in the family dynasty because he had no heir.

Since Nero's only true qualification as emperor was his pedigree, he extensively honored Agrippina and Claudius on the reverse of his coins. On the obverse, Nero's portrait reflects his gradual decline from a normal slim physique to an increasingly obese gluten. His bad behavior has made his coins some of the most fascinating to collectors and a must-have in any collection of gold coins of the ancient world. In numismatics, Nero is remembered for debasing the coinage to cover his extravagant expenditures. The Gold Aureus saw its first devaluation to 7.3 grams during his reign. Nero's coins were struck widely throughout the Roman Empire making them the most available coins of the Twelve Caesars.

VI · NERO

Did He Burn Rome to the Ground?

A Tyrant Known for His Unmatched Cruelty and Extravagance

The legend of Nero playing the fiddle during the burning of Rome is refuted historically given the fiddle did not exist in his era, but is a great metaphor for many Romans' beliefs that he caused the "Great Fire of Rome" that brought the city to its knees in order to clear land for his palace, the Domus Aurea. The adopted son of Claudius, he is known for his unmatched cruelty, often having Christians dipped in oil and burned alive in his garden for light in the dark hours of the night. He began the First Roman-Jewish War that ultimately destroyed the Second Temple of Jerusalem. His suicide in AD 68 plunged the Empire into a dark period known as the Year of the Four Emperors.

Nero was extremely narcissistic and had his coinage struck vastly throughout the Empire, making copper, silver, and gold coins of his reign among the most available of the Twelve Caesars. Even so, they are always in high demand due to his infamy.

This particular design type depicts Jupiter, god of the sky and thunder, also known as the king of the gods. Witness to oaths, he was seen as the key to the sacred trust of the Roman government and the people, thus implicating Nero as essential to the government and the people of Rome, as Jupiter was literally backing Nero. Extremely difficult to acquire in higher grades.

VII. SERGIUS GALBA.

GALBA was no way related to the Family of the Cæsars (that being Extinct in Nero;) but he was of one of the most noble and antient Families in Rome (the Servii.) He was noted for his Eloquence when young, and had something very promising in his Aspect. His advancement was foretold by Augustus; who saluted Galba, when a Youth, as one that should have a Taste of Imperial Power. From the Death of Augustus, to the Reign of Galba, was about 54 years; so that Galba did not come to the Throne till he was in his 73d year. He had born Offices under 4 Emperours successively, and had wonderfully preserv'd himself from the snares of Each Reign. He was declared Emperour, before the Death of Nero, by the Soldiers in Spain; and as soon as Nero was cut off, he was joyfully and unanimously set up at Rome. He was so unhappy as to bie very soon, the good opinion which was conceived of him whilst a private man. He gave way to a Cruel and Covetous Disposition, being under the Influence of Three very ill men, whom the People call'd his School-Masters. He Cut off a large Donative that was promis'd to the Army; declaring, that he chose his Soldiers, but he would never purchase them. This procur'd his Ruin, notwithstanding his strengthening himself by adopting Piso. The Armies in upper Germany revolted, and set up Otho; who sending his Soldiers to destroy Galba, they came upon him in the Forum, rushing in among the People and Senate, dispersing, or trampling them down till they reach'd Galba. They fell upon him very barbarously, and gave him many wounds, he offering them his Throat, and bidding them, if it was for the welfare of Rome, strike there. At last Cutting off his Head, they fix'd it upon a point of a Spear, and carried it about the Camp in contempt and Triumph. Many others were slaughter'd with him; and his adopted Son Piso was beheaded at the instigation of Otho. Galba reigned but 7 months, and as many days. In this Reign Sᵗ Clement is supposed to write his Epistle to the Corinthians. And the Jews, falling into horrid Factions, destroy'd one another.

~ GALBA ~

Nero's suicide in AD 68 ended the Julio-Claudian dynasty and resulted in another outbreak of civil war. Galba was the first emperor to rule during what is remembered as the "Year of the Four Emperors." This event initiated a period of political upheaval when several ambitious Romans vied to take control.

Born into a noble patrician family in Tarracina, in 3 BC, Servius Sulpicius Galba served in civil and military positions throughout the reigns of the Julio-Claudian emperors. While Galba was not related to the Julio-Claudians, he had a distinguished background and close ties to Augustus's wife Livia and to Claudius. Both Augustus and Tiberius are said to have told him that one day he would be at the head of the Roman world. While governor of the province of Africa, Galba became aware that Nero wanted him killed, so he rebelled and joined the military revolt against Nero.

At 73-years-old and the governor of Hispania Tarraconensis, a part of Spain, he received the support of the Spanish Legions, the Senate, and the Praetorian Guardsmen in Rome in his Imperial bid. Galba was proclaimed emperor by his troops, and the surviving members of the Roman Senate recognized his authority in July AD 68. He was able to ascend to the throne because of Nero's death that ended the Julio-Claudian dynasty.

He served as emperor for only seven months, in which time he alienated many supporters through a mixture of rigidity and stinginess. Galba arrived in Rome in October AD 68, and once in Rome, his rule was never secure, for he refused to bribe the soldiers and did not condone corruption. Galba also refused to pay the Praetorian Guard a reward for having deserted Nero. Finally, he adopted Lucius Piso as his successor instead of Otho, the former governor of Lusitania. His murder was arranged by Otho, an embittered compatriot who was willing to pay lavish bribes in his desire to succeed Galba. Otho won the support of the Praetorian Guard, who then killed both Galba and Piso in the Forum in public view.

In Galba's short reign, there were at least two coin types produced reflecting his time as emperor. He issued many coins which are surprisingly abundant, considering that his reign lasted only seven months. His coins were struck in Spain, Gaul, and Rome. His silver denarius coins can be readily found; however, bronze coins are a rare find, and Gold Aureus Coins of Galba are exceedingly rare. Locating problem-free specimens can be a major undertaking for collectors, but well worth the endeavor.

VII • Galba

XF Star • Strike: 5/5 • Surface: 4/5
~ FINE STYLE ~

The First Emperor of the
"Year of the Four Emperors"

SPQR/ OB/ C S (Senatus Populusque Romanus Ob Cives Servatos)
The Senate And the Roman People for Having Saved the Citizens

The Year of the Four Emperors lasted from early AD68 to late AD 69, and Galba was the first emperor during this time of Civil War. Although he had good intentions to restore state finances, the way he went about doing it enraged the populace and he was assassinated in AD 69 by the bribed Praetorian Guards at the request of Otho, who succeeded him. He was a man of great wealth and was unconnected by birth with any of the Caesars.

He was prophesied as early as the time of Augustus to be a man of future eminence in the Empire. He issued coins prolifically during his brief seven-month tenure. You can find his silver denarii with only mild difficulty, but collectors know his bronze and gold examples are a prize in high grade.

The Galba Aureus seen here is without a doubt, a prize for its type. With only 5 coins graded finer at NGC, and only 49 ever graded, this coin is an all-star. Perfect strike (5/5) and excellent surfaces (4/5) and designated Fine Style with its gorgeous classical motifs and brilliant solemn brooding portrait, you can see the look of a man, in such a chaotic time, who bears the weight of the Empire on his shoulders.

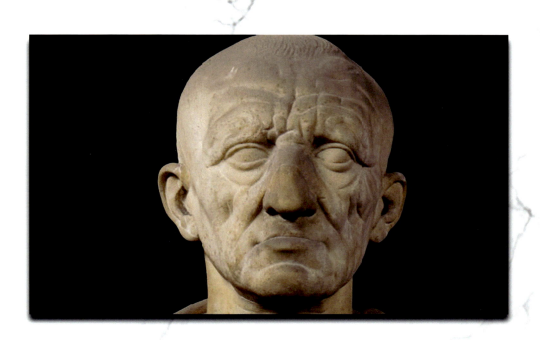

VIII. M. SYLVIUS OTHO.

OTHO *was of the Family of the Tuscan Kings, one of the Roman Eques, and one of Nero's Intimates. He made his Court to Galba upon his first advancement to the Empire, expecting to be adopted by him: But as soon as he saw Piso preferr'd before him, he thereupon resolved, by the help of his Soldiers, to seize the Empire for himself. Which he did in the manner before related (see Galba.) Otho was about 38 years old, when he came to the Throne; and was the first Emperour advanc'd to that honour by the Prætorian Guards. This gave occasion to their assuming the Authority (a thing of most pernicious Consequence) of Creating Emperours afterward. Vitellius, taking a like method of gaining the Roman Legions, was Created Emperor by those in Germany, whilst the Cohorts at Rome were for Otho. This divided the Roman Forces under two Heads, and three considerable Battels were fought by them in the Space of a few days. At length the Prætorian Cohorts were put to flight, and Otho at Brixellium yielded the day to Vitellius. Thus we find Power and Honour gain'd unjustly, Vanish'd Suddenly. Some Writers have made Otho took very Considerable in his manner of quitting the Empire. When the Soldiers on his side were still desirous to fight for him, He told them, "That he had rather Die, than Reign; Since he could never so much advance the Roman State by Wars and blood-shed, as by Sacrificing himself for the Peace of it." He profest not to blame the GODS, nor to Envy Vitellius's rising Glory, but, that he might preserve so many brave Soldiers and Fellow Citizens as appear'd in his Interest. He was therefore desirous to offer up his Life Voluntarily, and before it could be said he was Vanquish'd. Thus taking a Solemn Farewell of his whole Army, and desiring them to yield to Vitellius as soon as possible, he went into his Tent, and after a Sound Sleep took his Dagger and kill'd himself. Otho reigned 12 Weeks and 6 Days.*

~ OTHO ~

Marcus Salvius Otho was born in AD 32 and came from Etruscan aristocracy. He rose to prominence as a courtier in Nero's imperial court. Living among the ruling class, he was one of the wild young aristocrats in Nero's entourage. Nero forced him to divorce his wife Poppaea, so he could have her for himself, then sent Otho to govern distant Lusitania which is modern-day Portugal.

While in Lusitania and hoping to become Galba's successor, Otho joined Galba's revolt against Nero in AD 68. When Galba adopted Lucius Piso instead, his hopes to be designated as his successor were thwarted so Otho prepared to seize power himself, and he conspired with the Praetorian Guard to kill the emperor. Galba and Piso were murdered, and Otho was acclaimed emperor on January 15, AD 69.

Otho was one of Rome's least impressive emperors and would only reign a mere three months (January 15 - April 16, AD 69). During this short time, the legions on the German frontier proclaimed their general Vitellius as emperor, with troops which were already moving toward Italy to march on Rome. The impatient Otho should have waited, but rather he insisted on quick action and summoned his Danube legions to march out to meet the Vitellian forces, determined to bring it to an end as quickly as possible. Vitellius' legions were poorly supplied but stronger, and they had reinforcements on their way. Vitellius' legions were winning the battle, and Otho saw no escape. To avoid more bloodshed and spare Rome further conflict, he killed himself before he could be defeated on the battlefield and captured.

Even though Otho only ruled for three months, the efficiency of the Roman mint produced many coins of Otho coinage in that brief period. Otho was vain about his appearance and wore an obvious toupee to cover his bald head, a distinctive feature of his coin obverse portrait. The reverse of some types features the winged figure of Victory surrounded by the inscription VICTORIA OTHONIS which translates to "Victory of Otho". His Gold Aureus coins are exceedingly rare in any condition and are a major cornerstone to any ancient collection. Most collectors are willing to accept any example to fill in the collection, but the astute collector who remains patient, seeking problem-free specimens, have been handsomely rewarded in the past.

VIII · Otho

XF · Strike: 5/5 · Surface: 3/5

"It is Far More Just to Perish One For All, Than Many For One"

Otho spoke those words to his army before retiring to his study the night he committed suicide by stabbing himself with a dagger. An unimaginable act in earlier time, previous emperors were far too narcissistic to have done such a thing, caring about themselves before their subjects. Otho is a complex figure that history has placed in a more favorable light since his death.

His initial rise to power was by capitalizing on Galba's refusal to honor his offer to pay the Praetorian guards with gold, which led to his assassination. As with Galba, the coinage of Otho presents a sincere challenge to the astute collector, and all coins issued in his name are in very high demand. This civil war emperor struck no bronze, so collectors must compete for surviving silver and gold pieces. His denarii are quite scarce, and his aurei are extremely rare and difficult to find. He served for just three months as the second emperor of the "Year of the Four Emperors."

This Otho Aureus features a right-facing head of Otho on the obverse and Securitas, goddess of security, on the reverse. This is a superb example of an Otho Aureus, with a perfect strike and almost flawless surface for this issue. The second most elusive of the Twelve Caesars and a must own in any grade.

IX. Aᴜʟʟᴜs Vɪᴛᴇʟʟɪᴜs.

Vɪᴛᴇʟʟɪᴜs the Roman General, having Conquered Otho, was pronounc'd Emperour by the Senate with the usual Solemnities.
He severely punish'd the prætorian Cohorts who had been Instruments in Galba's Death, and Otho's Advancement. Commanding that
120 of them who were most guilty should be Executed. This honourable Act gave hope of Vitellius's proving a good Prince: But he soon
gave the reins to his Vices in a most detestable manner. He gave up himself to Luxury and Excess, together with his Family and Soldiers,
who were tolerated in all kinds of Wickedness. He govern'd State matters at the Discretion of a Player, and Chariot Driver,
especially of Asiaticus his Freed-man. He was such a prodigal Glutton, that he had 2000 dishes of Fish, and 7000 of Fowls,
served to his Table at one Supper. He was so Cruel that he would kill any person, and for any cause whatsoever. He was
suspected of murdering his Mother. He became so stupid by his sottish, vicious Life, that he forgot all things past, and regarded nothing
present or to come; insomuch that Historians tell us, if others had not own'd him dayly to be the Prince, he himself would have
forgot it. All discourse and rumour of war was strictly forbidden, not only at Court, but throughout the City, till these wretched
Fortifications of mirth and sottishness were destroy'd by the comeing of Vespasian's Forces. After many provocations and Skirmishes, those
Forces entred the City of Rome, and committed grievous outrages. They pull'd Vitellius out of a hole in the Palace, where he
thought to lie hid, till some Terms were made for him. They tied his hands behind him, cast an Halter about his neck, dragg'd
him half naked into the Forum. Abused him with many Words, and kill'd him at last with many Blows. Then after the fashion of
Traytors, they threw him into the Tyber. He reign'd 8 months 5 days.

~ VITELLIUS ~

Aulus Vitellius was born in AD 14, the son of the Emperor Claudius's colleague as censor, Lucius Vitellius, who was consul three times. In his youth, he was one of the noble companions of Tiberius' retirement on Capri, and there befriended Caligula, who shared in his passion for chariot racing and games of dice. Vitellius achieved wealth and influence as a part of the imperial court under Caligula, Claudius, and Nero. After Nero's death, Galba appointed Vitellius governor of Lower Germany in AD 68 and to command the legions on the German frontier. He made himself popular with the soldiers by outrageous extravagance, generosity, and excessive good nature, which soon proved fatal to military order and discipline. Nevertheless, he defeated Otho's forces and occupied Rome in June, AD 69.

Vitellius challenged Otho for the imperial office, and the superiority of his army drove Otho to suicide. On January 2, AD 69, he was elevated to the position of emperor by the ambition of his troops, more than his own. Vitellius proved himself to be a perpetual underachiever, and only lasted eight months as emperor. He is remembered as a drunken glutton, feasting up to four times a day on costly imported delicacies and endless expensive banquets leaving little time to govern.

The new reign of Vitellius was challenged almost immediately by Vespasian, a Roman general who since AD 67, had been waging war in the province of Judaea. As Vespasian advanced on Rome, Vitellius offered no resistance to the challenge and tried to resign, but his troops would not allow it. He was hunted down, dragged out of hiding, and driven to the Gemonian stairs, where he was tortured and beheaded on December 22, AD 69. His head was paraded around Rome, and his body was then flung down the stairs and attacked by Rome's residents, who dragged his body by a hook into the Tiber river. Being executed and abused on the stairs was a matter of great shame and dishonor for the dead.

Vitellius mainly issued Denarii and Aurei since there were still many Nero and Galba coins in circulation. Despite his short reign, he issued many different coin types, some with new propaganda, and others traditional, with reverse types that honor the loyalty of the army. Coins of Vitellius are among the scarcest in the Twelve Caesars series, only Otho's total coinage output was smaller. He is the second scarcest of the Twelve Caesars overall, but only the fifth scarcest for collectors who are devoted to building denarii sets. His Gold Aureus coins are quite scarce today and very difficult to find in high grade, with problem-free surfaces or edges.

IX · Vitellius

CHOICE XF STAR · STRIKE: 5/5 · SURFACE: 4/5

The Drunken Glutton Who Lost His Head

Vitellius served for eight months as the third emperor of the "Year of the Four Emperors." His rise from politician and army commander to emperor was swift, undoubtedly due to the rash and unstable state of Rome in civil war. Known as an extravagant glutton, under his rule Rome became the bizarre scene of excessive violence in the streets and lavish feasts at night. While in the act of submitting his resignation as emperor, he was murdered by Vespasian's troops and his head was paraded around Rome. His last words were "Yet I was once your emperor."

Vitellius managed to produce a sizable coinage in a short period by resuming the striking of bronze coins. The vast majority of these bronzes can be found in heavily circulated grades and his gold coins are extremely difficult to find in problem-free grades above Very Fine.

It goes without saying that this specimen of Vitellius Aureus in Choice XF Star condition is quite an achievement. With a stunning eye-catching portrait that exhibits beautiful surfaces under the light, the luster blazes for this Vitellius with awesome eye-appeal. It features great detail in the hair as well as the cheek bones, with a prominent forehead and nose depicted in this particular design type. The legends are completely visible, and the reverse surpasses the quality generally seen on a Choice XF. Only 5 Finer at NGC.

X D VESPASIANUS AUGUSTUS.

VESPASIAN *was of the family of the Flavij, therefore called Flavius Vespasian. He was General of the Forces in Germany and Britain, then Governour in Africa; and was sent by Nero, notwithstanding his Prejudices against him, to manage the wars in Judæa. He was first declared Emperor by the Legions at Alexandria; but was so averse to accept the Title, that the Soldiers gathered about him with their drawn Sword and threatned his immediate Death if he refus'd the Empire. Upon such a violent determination of the matter, a part of the Army was ordered to march directly to Rome, where they soon became Masters; and putting Vitellius to an infamous Death, the Senate was soon brought to declare Vespasian Emperour. They also confirm'd the Kingdom to him a Hereditary some part of the Lex Regia, by which things were then settled, is yet extant. After several months stay at Alexandria, VESPASIAN set sail for Italy, and was received at Rome with the greatest magnificence, and the utmost transports of Joy. He was about 50, years of age when he ascended the Throne. He left y management of the Jewish Wars to his Son Titus, making him a Partner of all his cares and Honours. He rais'd considerable sums of money by a Tax upon Urine, excepting whichever taxe source any mean or little thing in his Adminis-tration. One of our Historians gives him this Character He was a Prince of great Wisdom, moderation, and modesty; next to Iulius Cæsar in Wisand to Augustus in Peace; rais'd by Providence to restore a sinking Empire; and one whom Pliny said, that Greatness and Majesty had changed nothing in him, but only to make his Power of doing good answerable to his Will. He was the 2.d Roman Emperour that died a natural Death, and the 1.st that was succeeded by his own Son. He died of a Flux in the 69.th year of his age, being set upon his feet when he found himself expiring, and declaring that an Emperour ought to die in such a Posture. Thus he concluded a laborious Reign of about 10, years. In this Reign Titus besieged the famous City of Jerusalem, and took it. the Iews Temple is also demolish'd. The Temple of Peace was dedicated. Several Provinces were reduc'd to the Roman Power. There were great Earthquakes in some places, and a grievous Plague in Rome. Among the Christians arose several Heresies, particularly those of Menander, Ebion, and Cerinthus.*

~ VESPASIAN ~

After the chaotic 'Year of the Four Emperors' ran its course and the killing of Vitellius, the pathway was cleared for Vespasian to emerge as Rome's new emperor. Born with humble beginnings in AD 9, Vespasian was the son of Flavius Sabinus, a Roman knight who had been a tax collector, and his mother, Vespasia Polla, belonged to the equestrian order in society. In his early life, Vespasian was somewhat overshadowed by his older brother, Flavius Sabinus, who rose to hold an important military command, and then entered the Senate under Nero. Vespasian married Flavia Domitilla, who was not a Roman citizen, with whom he had a daughter and two sons, Titus and Domitian, both of whom later became emperors.

Over the years, Vespasian rose through the ranks of civil and military service and distinguished himself during the invasion of Britain in AD 43. In AD 67, Nero sent him to crush a revolt in Judaea which escalated into the Jewish War that dragged on until the year 73, finally being concluded by Vespasian's son, Titus. On July 1, AD 69, the legions proclaimed Vespasian emperor at Alexandria. On December 20, Vespasian arrived in Rome, Emperor Vitellius was dragged to his death, and the Senate confirmed Vespasian's accession to the throne. This brought the tumultuous 'Year of the Four Emperors' to a close.

Ending the period of civil war, Vespasian became the first emperor since the Julio-Claudians to establish a stable dynasty. He launched a building plan and restoration of the city of Rome at a time when its wealth had been depleted by civil wars and irresponsible leadership. Vespasian was a man of great energy, humility and common sense, the best emperor of Rome since Augustus. Known for his frugality and sense of humor, Vespasian established himself as one of Rome's most competent generals and dutiful emperors. Under his reign, the people of the Roman world enjoyed 10-years of political stability and economic prosperity. Before dying of natural causes on June 23, AD 79, at 69 years old, Vespasian ensured that the Senate would allow his son Titus to succeed him as emperor, beginning the Flavian dynasty, which included Vespasian and his two sons, Titus and Domitian, who ruled Rome for 27 years, from AD 69 through AD 96.

Vespasian was responsible for the economic and military recovery of Rome and is justly regarded as one of the greatest Roman emperors. He struck many coins in gold, silver, and copper, in the process of restoring prosperity to the Empire. There were many different and interesting design types, from military conquests to coins that depict his sons. As a very popular emperor, his coins are highly prized, with many available in high-quality condition making them very desirable for collectors.

X • VESPASIAN

TWELVE CAESARS
Vespasian, AD 69-79
AV Aureus (7.38g)
rv Ceres std. hldg. grain
ears & torch
3990590-001

Ch MS
Strike: 5/5
Surface: 5/5

NGC ANCIENTS

CHOICE MS • STRIKE: 5/5 • SURFACE: 5/5

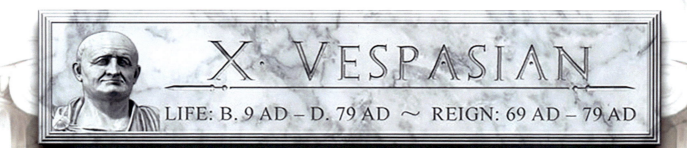
The Final Ruler in the "Year of the Four Emperors"

The Founder of the Flavian Dynasty, and the tenth in the line of the Twelve Caesars, Emperor Vespasian ended a Civil War, and was the final ruler of the tumultuous Year of the Four Emperors. His tenure brought about a time of peace for 27 years.

He hailed from an equestrian family with political ties. As a military commander, he had immense success during the First Jewish-Roman War and in Britain. He was responsible for several important architectural projects, most notably the beginning of construction on the Roman Colosseum (also called the Flavian Amphitheater), as Vespasian had a love for gladiatorial games.

Coins struck during his reign served as propaganda throughout the Empire, depicting images of military victory and peace. He died in AD 79 of intestinal illness after a long and successful career as emperor.

In Choice Mint State condition, this coin is truly the cream of the crop while featuring Ceres, goddess of agriculture, fertility, and motherly relationships on the reverse, holding grains in one hand and a torch in the other. No photography can do it justice, for when this coin is under the light, its fields glow with radiant luster. Truly a magnificent example of a Vespasian aureus.

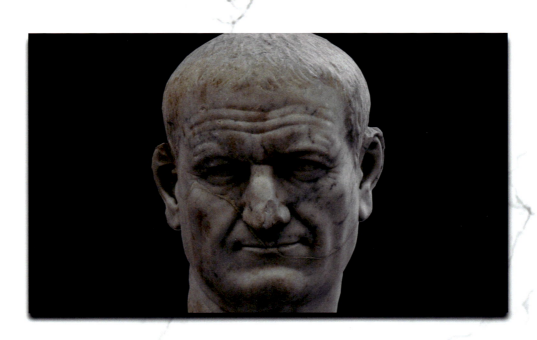

XI. D. TITUS VESPASIANUS

TITUS was the eldest Son of Vespasian; a Person of uncommon excellencies and accomplishments both as to his Body, and Mind. He serv'd in many wars, and particularly the Iewish, with great renown. At his taking Ierusalem he wept when he conquered. He was famous in several expeditions. And was greatly celebrated for Wisdom in discharging several offices of state. He was universally received as Emperour upon the death of Vespasian. He was charg'd with several vices in his private life, and with some severity in his natural temper; but his conduct in publick was such, that he was styled the Darling and delight of mankind. He was 39 years old when he came to the Throne; and being advis'd to tread in his Fathers steps, he did so, and became a most excellent Prince. He was so tender of his Peoples Happiness, that his usual saying was, none ought to go sad from his Presence. If a day pass'd without doing good to some body, he would lament it as a lost day. He would receive no accusations against those that spake evil of him, declaring; that so long as he did nothing that deserv'd Reproach, he valued not lies. He was a great Enemy to the Extorters and Promoters of Penal laws, causing them to be banish'd Rome. He forgave such as were convicted of Treason, in a manner that was enough to subdue any Heart: And did every thing that kindness could do to conquer the traiterous ambitious Temper of his Brother Domitian. But, in that unhappy Instance, his goodness prov'd ineffectual. He is suppos'd to have been poison'd by Domitians procurement, when he had reign'd but two years two months, and 20 days. He was taken away as a Prince too deserving for so corrupt an age. In this reign there was a vast eruption of Vesuvius, by which the famous Pliny was suffocated, after he had written his Natural History, and dedicated it to Titus. Fires, Plagues, and other calamities happen'd in Rome, in which the Goodness and Humanity of Titus were wonderfully signaliz'd. Agricola began his conquests in Brittain. And the Wars of the Iews were written by Iosephus, and put into the publick Library.

~ TITUS ~

Titus Flavius Vespasianus was born in Rome on December 30, AD 39, the oldest son of the future emperor, Vespasian, and older brother of future emperor, Domitian. Since childhood, Titus had been a part of the highest echelon of Roman society. He grew up with Emperor Claudius' son, Britannicus, raised in the imperial court, and shared education and military training. By the time his father, Vespasian received his Judaean command, Titus was ready to lead his own legions to suppress the Jewish Revolt. Titus was at his father's side in Judaea, when Vespasian returned to Rome to assert his claim for the imperial throne, Titus took command, captured Jerusalem in the face of fanatical and heroic resistance, and destroyed and sacked its temple in AD 70, bringing the Jewish War to an end.

Before he became emperor, Titus was widely criticized for his alleged cruelty, heavy drinking, and his affair with the Jewish Queen Berenice, which ended once he became emperor. After Jerusalem fell, Titus returned to Rome to aid his father in government until AD 79 when his father passed, Titus became the second emperor of the Flavian dynasty at nearly 40 years old. Like Vespasian, Titus was a capable military leader, and he proved to be a competent emperor as well. He retained most of his father's economic and political practices but cultivated a milder, more liberal image. He refused to act violently against people who plotted against him.

Titus was handsome, charming, and generous, however, generous to a fault, which depleted the treasury. He enjoyed excellent relations with the Senate and was popular with the people for the lavish games he put on. During his reign he finished what would be the most enduring reminder of his family; the Colosseum in Rome, known as the Flavian Amphitheater, which his father began in AD 70 and Titus dedicated in AD 80. Titus' reign was tainted with several catastrophes; a great fire in Rome, devastating plagues, and the cataclysmic eruption of Mt. Vesuvius, which buried half the towns in the Bay of Naples, including Pompeii in AD 79. Titus proved to be exceptionally generous with the survivors.

Titus was not greatly popular during his lifetime, but his reputation rose steadily during the ensuing tyranny of his brother Domitian. Just two years into his reign on September 13, AD 81, he suddenly became ill and died from poisoning, possibly by his brother, Domitian. In his last moments, he drew back the curtains and gazed up at the sky with bitter complaints that life was being undeservedly taken from him. Allegedly, his last words before passing were "I have made but one mistake." Upon his death, his younger brother, Domitian, succeeded him, whose first act as emperor was to deify his brother Titus. He was mourned as an emperor with the best interests of his people at heart.

Titus' accomplishments are recognized by collectors around the world who are drawn to collect his coins. Despite his short reign as emperor, Titus struck many coins as Caesar. His most famous coin is a very rare bronze sestertius depicting the Colosseum, the massive stadium built with the loot from the Jewish War. It is possible today to acquire a gold, silver, and copper coin of this good-natured emperor for a good value.

XI · TITUS

AU · STRIKE: 5/5 · SURFACE: 3/5
~ FINE STYLE ~

The First Son of a 'Twelve Caesar'-
He Completed the Roman Colosseum

In 2007 a new list of the Seven Wonders of the World was created, adding the Colosseum in Rome to the list for the first time. Begun under his father, the Colosseum was completed under Titus. This landmark tells the story of the days of the gladiator and is frequented by millions of visitors annually. It is today one of the most iconic global landmarks and the grand symbol of ancient Rome.

Titus was the son of Vespasian and was the first son of a 'Twelve Caesar' to rule. As the second emperor of the Flavian Dynasty, Titus gained immense notoriety as a military commander serving under his father in the First Jewish-Roman War. After ruling for just two short years, Titus fell ill and died ostensibly of natural causes in AD 81.

Issued as Caesar, this Aureus featuring Pax, the goddess of peace, on the reverse. Holding an olive branch, she is comfortably seated as she gestures hopefully toward an era of prosperity for Rome. The coin features a handsome bust of Titus, with excellent details of his jawline and facial features. This coin depicts the legends very clearly and exhibits a perfect strike (5/5) and a solid surface grade of (3/5). This beautiful Titus Aureus was designated as Fine Style for its tasteful beauty and refined artistic style.

XII. FLAVIUS DOMITIANUS.

DOMITIAN *was so called from* Domitilla *his Mother, being the younger Son of* Vespasian. *As he came to the Empire by poys'ning one of the best of Princes, (his brother* Titus,*) so he prov'd himself one of the Vilest and worst of men. He pass'd his Youth disgracefully. In the beginning of his Reign, he shew'd a very mean and trifling Spirit being much taken up in a private Gallery with Catching Flies, and pricking them through with a Bodkin. One of his Attendants, therefore, being ask'd if any body was with* Cæsar, *answered,* no not so much as a flie. *He caused his statue to be made of Gold, and to be Worshipped; and ordered that the Title of* GOD *and our* LORD *should be given to him. Upon the smallest Surmizes, he murdered his Nobles, and some of his own Kindred. Confiscations and Banishments were Favours from him. But his Guilt made him timerous out of measure; so that the place where he was wont to abide, was set round with a bright stone called* Phengites, *(something like a Looking-Glass in its reflecting Images) that he might see if any one came behind him. However, the thing so justly feared by him, at last came upon him, being murdered, and his dead Carcase disgracefully used; his Scutcheons also, and Images being defaced by order of the* Senate. *He reigned 15 years and 5 days.   In this reign* Agricola *reduced all* Brittain *to the* Roman *Power: which gain'd him so great Fame that 'tis supposed* Domitian, *not able to bear it rewarded him with a Dose of Poyson.* Cornelia *was buried alive for Incontinency.* Apollonius Tyanæus *perform'd several Musical Tricks.* Quintilian *publish'd his Rhetorick.* Josephus *finish'd his Antiquities of the* Jews. *The sect of the* Nazarenes, *and the Heresie of the* Nicolaitans *arose. There was a second general Persecution of the* Christians, *in which* S[t]. JOHN *was banished to* Patmos, *and there wrote his Revelation. The Family of the* Herods *Extinct.*

~ DOMITIAN ~

The last of the 'Twelve Caesars' was Domitian, born Titus Flavius Domitianus, on Oct. 24, AD 51. He was the third and last emperor in the Flavian Dynasty and the youngest, less favored, son of Vespasian. As a youth, he remained in Rome studying rhetoric and literature while his father and brother campaigned in the African provinces and Judaea. Domitian lacked any military experience, and did not gain Titus' education or experience, nor acquire political savvy or respect towards the Senate. He did, however, hold several honorary consulships and priest-hoods, but had no important imperial position or office in his father's or brother's Imperial Court.

Domitian ascended to emperor upon Titus' death from a sudden fever and illness, possibly brought on by poison. He was about 30 years old when he succeeded his older brother as emperor of Rome in AD 81. Domitian was kind and charitable in his early years and ruled moderately, but not successfully at first with Rome falling into economic depression which resulted in a currency devaluation. His attempts to reconstruct and embellish the city by erecting many new buildings strained the state's finances. In the later years of his reign, he revealed a rigid, cruel streak. He was aggressive militarily and led daring campaigns, personally taking part in battles in Germany attempting to win the kind of glory his father and brother had earned in Judaea. He was an unsympathetic emperor whose life was framed by the envy he felt toward his older brother, Titus.

As emperor, Domitian was hated by the aristocracy, and became somewhat of a tyrannical dictator, demanding the Senate refer to him as "Master and God." In his contempt and fears of conspiracy against him, he had many senators murdered. He became suspicious to the point of paranoia, and even his close friends and household servants no longer felt safe and conspired to murder him. On September 18, AD 96, Domitian was murdered by his wife's steward in a palace coup, bringing an end to the period of the "Twelve Caesars." After his assassination, the Senate had his memory erased, pronouncing, 'damnatio memoriae,' the condemnation of memory.

His 15-year reign was the longest since that of Tiberius. His coinage was prolific, probably the most abundant of the of all the 'Twelve Caesars' coinage. His silver denarius coins are available in most grades and represent a great value for those inspired by Roman history, however, pleasing specimens of his gold and copper coins are surprisingly hard to find.

XII · DOMITIAN

CHOICE AU • STRIKE: 5/5 • SURFACE: 4/5
~ FINE STYLE ~

Paranoid Younger Brother of Titus and Last of the Twelve Caesars

Domitian, the last of the Twelve Caesars, restored the economy by revaluing Roman coinage, rebuilding the city of Rome, and fortifying the border defenses of the Empire. He felt immense envy towards his older brother, Titus, and had a great desire to conquer Germany in an effort to achieve military fame, as in the end, Titus had received all the glory for the successes in Judea. Domitian became deeply paranoid after learning of an astrological prediction about his death at "approximately noon" and would become extremely reclusive around this time each day. He is said to have had a dream just days before his assassination in which the goddess Minerva came to him and told him she could no longer protect him.

The specimen represented here is perfectly centered with a complete strike (Strike: 5/5) and centering on the legends, with an exceptional surface (4/5) and every bit of eye appeal and originality expected of a Choice AU specimen. You can practically stare into his soul when you gaze upon the portrait. The obverse features the laureate head of Domitian, and the reverse is a commemorative issue representing Rome's past conquests. This particular coin is depicting the Roman goddess of hope, Spes, advancing forward, a notion of hope depicted to say that Domitian will bring hope to the Empire.

TWELVE CAESARS — MS★
Julius Caesar, d. 44 BC
AV Aureus (8.08g)
c.46 BC A. Hirtius praetor
obv Pietas, rv
3987321-002

TWELVE CAESARS — Ch AU
Augustus, 27 BC-AD 14
AV Aureus (7.77g)
Lugdunum
rv Gaius & Lucius Caesars
Strike: 5/5
Surface: 3/5
Fine Style
3987844-001

TWELVE CAESARS — MS
Tiberius, AD 14-37
AV Aureus (7.71g)
Lugdunum
rv Livia as Pax
Strike: 5/5
Surface: 3/5
4276183-004

TWELVE CAESARS — AU
Caligula, AD 37-41
AV Aureus (7.90g)
rv radiate hd. of Augustus
or Tiberius betw. stars
Strike: 5/5
Surface: 4/5
3990551-001

TWELVE CAESARS — Ch MS
Claudius, AD 41-54
AV Aureus (7.78g)
rv SPQR PP OB C S
in oak wreath
Strike: 5/5
Surface: 5/5
3990575-001

TWELVE CAESARS — AU
Nero, AD 54-68
AV Aureus (7.23g)
rv Jupiter std.
Strike: 5/5
Surface: 4/5
Fine Style
3987843-002

TWELVE CAESARS — XF★
Galba, AD 68-69
AV Aureus (7.34g)
rv SPQR OB CS
in oak wreath
Strike: 5/5
Surface: 4/5
Fine Style
3990570-001

TWELVE CAESARS — XF
Otho, AD 69
AV Aureus (7.30g)
rv Securitas stg.
Strike: 5/5
Surface: 3/5
3987337-001

TWELVE CAESARS — Ch XF★
Vitellius, AD 69
AV Aureus (7.35g)
rv Concordia std.
ex M&M 37 (1968) 300?
Strike: 5/5
Surface: 4/5
3988900-001

TWELVE CAESARS — Ch MS
Vespasian, AD 69-79
AV Aureus (7.38g)
rv Ceres std. hldg. grain
ears & torch
Strike: 5/5
Surface: 5/5
3990590-001

TWELVE CAESARS — AU
Titus, AD 79-81
AV Aureus (7.29g)
issued as Caesar
rv Pax std.
Strike: 5/5
Surface: 3/5
Fine Style
3987835-002

TWELVE CAESARS — Ch AU
Domitian, AD 81-96
AV Aureus (7.24g)
issued as Caesar
rv Spes advancing
Strike: 5/5
Surface: 4/5
Fine Style
3987825-002

~ SUMMARY ~

The Twelve Caesars Coin Collection captures the lives of the Roman Empire's first twelve Roman emperors, the men who began an empire that reigned over a golden age of human civilization. Each of the coins in the Twelve Caesars collection represents a different emperor of Rome spanning from the time of Julius Caesar beginning in 49 BC, until the reign of the last Flavian emperor, Domitian, in AD 96.

The feeling of holding ancient coins from the time of Twelve Caesars brings history to life. Due to their limited supply and historical significance, these coins of ancient Rome have steadily increased in value over time and have, with astute buying, provided a tremendous private storage of wealth.

I. **Julius Caesar's** fame and accomplishments make his gold extremely difficult to find. Owning one of these coins is one of the most prestigious accomplishments for numismatic collectors.

II. **Augustus** struck coins in abundance, yet few have survived in high grade. Many design types were produced under his rule, inspiring collectors to make an attempt at acquiring them all.

III. **Tiberius** Caesar is known for his conservative growth of the Empire. Demand for his coins is usually high because they were minted around the same time period as Christ's crucifixion.

IV. **Caligula's** coins are exceedingly rare and are always in high demand. The rare availability of this coin can sometimes make it a stumbling block for collectors looking to complete their set.

V. The coins of **Claudius** are frequently in high demand. His silver and gold coins are rare and hard to find and most buyers seek portrait bronzes for their collection.

VI. **Nero's** coins were struck widely throughout the Roman Empire making them the most available. Even so, demand is high due to his infamy as one of Rome's most ruthless Caesar.

VII. **Galba** only ruled for seven months but issued many coins. His silver denarius coins can be found with little difficulty, however, his bronze and gold coins are a rare find.

VII. **Otho** struck no Imperial bronzes which leave collectors with the option of either a silver denarius or a gold aureus. His denarii are scarce, and his aurei are extremely difficult to find.

IX. **Vitellius** managed to produce an abundance of coinage in a short period. Additionally, he resumed the striking of bronzes. Though available, his coins are difficult to find in high grade.

X. Coins struck during **Vespasian's** reign served as propaganda throughout the Empire, depicting images of military victory and peace. He struck large quantities of gold, silver, and copper coins.

XI. Despite his short reign as emperor, **Titus** struck many coins which makes it possible to acquire gold, silver, or copper coins of this good-natured emperor at a reasonable price.

XII. **Domitian's** silver denarius coins represent the best value; nice examples of his gold and copper coins are surprisingly hard to find.